The Wrecks of Eden

The Wrecks of Eden

Catherine Owen

Wolsak and Wynn · Toronto

Typeset in Goudy Old Style.
Printed in Canada by The Coach House Printing Company, Toronto.
Front cover art: Maurice Spira
Cover design: The Coach House Printing Company, Toronto
Author's photograph: Chad Norman

The author thanks the Canada Council for the Arts for their support.

The publisher gratefully acknowledges
the generous support of the
Canada Council for the Arts
and the Ontario Arts Council.

The Canada Council   Le Conseil des Arts   ONTARIO ARTS COUNCIL
   for the Arts   du Canada   CONSEIL DES ARTS DE L'ONTARIO

Poems included in this book have appeared previously in *Antigonish Review*,
Canadian Forum, *Canadian Literature*, *Fiddlehead*, *Quarter Moon Quarterly*, *Queen's
Quarterly*, *The New Orphic Review*, and *Wascana Review*.

Wolsak and Wynn Publishers Ltd
192 Spadina Avenue, Suite 315
Toronto, Ontario
Canada M5T 2C2

National Library of Canada Cataloguing in Publication Data
Owen, Catherine
        The wrecks of Eden
Poems.
ISBN 0-919897-80-0
I. Title
PS8579.W43W74 2001   C811'.54   C2001-902392-8
PR9199.3.O94W74 2001

... a paradise was created, as out of the wrecks of Eden
—Percy Bysshe Shelley

Death is one thing, an end to birth something else
—Gary Snyder

Contents

The Lost

Antenatal (a memo)

Give birth to an extinct species, aid
its lost blueprint to reformulate

in the miracle of meiosis. Let the
diploid cell of a dodo enact division

in your uterus, an auroch expand the fetal
sac with softly-cloven hooves. Feel the kicks

of bison bonasus, the undulations as a hare-
lipped sucker fish turns in the amniotic inlet.

Hear the Cretan owl hoot in the delivery room,
a passenger pigeon coo as the umbilical cord

is cut. Have a caesarean section for a mammoth,
an episiotomy if it will ease the heath hen

back into the world. Abandon human conception.
Let your womb become parous with absent

forms of life. Bear down for the echoed breaths,
nurse the squandered, diverse mouths.

The christening

Viola cryana, a small, wild pansy, became extinct
in a Seine, France rock quarry in 1950.

Bathing the child in the dimming room,
    we know he is no longer Adam.

There is no return from Newton, Bacon
    or the atom bomb; Eden was never innocence

but a baptism of tameness in Noah's Flood.
    On the apple of his genitals, a sightless stone

mason and a flower's moniker tussle. His mother lies
    excavated, the umbilicus a tendril on the ground.

His brow is a fist of tenderness. We name him after extinctions.
    He wails in his lexicon of absence.

The Dodo

Extinct on Reunion Isl., c. 1790.
        unassuming things that hold a silent station in this world
                                        —William Wordsworth

If there is a dubious glamour
to being extinct, then surely the Dodo

is the Mae West of the lost.
In youth, it was the only creature I knew

that was no longer alive, except
in images, as almost a poster beast

for the vanished, with its thick, curved
beak, waterfall of tail feathers and stubby,

inert wings. Or inside the language, in expressions
such as *don't be such a dodo*, or *dull as a dodo* :

unflattering epithets spawned by inept
observations; sailors intent on meat who mocked

the peace-keeping birds squatting passively
before their guns, as their hounds decimated

the oval silence of eggs. *It deserved to be exterminated,*
they later said, *just sitting there like that,*

doing nothing. As reminiscence of this flightless dove,
I prefer Sir Thomas Herbert's words, who

described the eyes of the last-seen Dodo as
like to diamonds, round and rowling.

Severance package

Others likely went missing in the one loss
: inchworms, perhaps, or ticks, beetles with glabrous
backs, a certain kind of burrowing rat, a type of moss,
a tint of blood, feather's sheen or bitter taste

—none accounted for, of course, only the large
absences were stuffed, grieved or sketched—
some in decaying texts, their backdrops hued & rigged
to look Elysian, not a once-paradise, plundered for wretched

appetites. Take the Calvaria tree, for instance, which
vanished not long after the Dodo, to little notice.
Its seeds were germinated, not by chance, but
in the Dodo's gizzard, erupting like a poultice

on the earth from a bolus of digested fruit. With
the last Dodo shot, the tree became scarce, then ceased
to show its gnarled pate, bark and roots on any of the fertile
islands the sailors had rampaged.

Gone the Dodo, famed bird, the Calvaria tree, its mate,
and how many others unnamed?

The quickest extinction

The passenger pigeon, common until 1910, became extinct in 1914.

9 boxcars hired for the kill.
48 hunters wired by telegraph:

                                    flocks of thousands sighted

Loaves & fishes
divided among the masses

> So many birds
> their bodies blocked out the light,
> beaks parted in a swell of cooing,
> pinions beating the Minnesota summer
> into hail sounds...

Go ye forth brethren
& multiply

> Hunters on their guts in the scrub
> grass, tumescent rifles pointed at squabs,
> plump, iridescent shapes glittering with flight,
> shooting, shooting again. Re-loading prowess, cowardice.

Great swarms
of locusts, milk
& honey flowing

> At hour's end they counted eight thousand blood-
> damp birds between them, plus the smooth,
> doomed eggs scavenged from derelict nests high
> in the forks of alders. Couldn't believe their fortune.

Hosts & hosts
of angels on
the head of a pin

        Halfway home, the kill heaped in boxcars,
        the train broke down. By the time the brakeman
        had figured out what was wrong, the birds
        had begun to rot, flesh reeking in the bright noon sun.
        Nothing for it. The corpses were chucked, in a crude
        re-enactment of flight, down ravines, into ditches.

We lied when we got back,
said we'd been misled, there
were no birds.

        Pigeon bones, becoming pictographs on hills.

"The forest of Rapa...had one hundred species of land snail.
None survived the total destruction of the vegetation."
                                        —Balouet & Alibert

soft equus
fetus-shaped
eyes on the apex of reins

tapping absence.
no shell is coiled deeply enough
to vanish in.

male imprints shatter
the pinnacle—luminous
as past labyrinths—reduce

it to a rubble of map-born
ruins, scarcely clinging
to a flesh gelatinous

and silent.
one hundred species
on the heel of machinery,

history-shards
beneath cities.

Lazarus-Quagga

Who would will return to this cage-awaiting time?
Not this zebra's cousin, half-imprisoned by markings,
dwindled by hunting, though cloven-swift once
and copious as calves.

From a stuffed replica of wilderness, a taxidermist
(bent on fame) grapples with echoes of hair and blood,
gene pools uninhabited since the quagga last lived.
To what end the renewal of this severed code, the

resurrection of cracked sand? Like children, we dream
whole a slain time with coins and candle flames
(death never a final utterance even when the nix
is our own doing). We muster an assemblage of tools,

snippers for bindings, yet the blueprint grips its stone,
resists our deciphering. Stumped on how to inhabit a land
without loss, we invent machines to imagine birth.
Whose four walls will kill this found-again beast

—this quagga with the foretold skin?

A century's resort

for the Israeli gerbil, extinct in 1986 after a housing complex
was built on its seaside habitat

on the sand accents
of an older way of living,

glitzy blueprints
attain fruition.

the floor plans
are spacious.

each buyer is to have
gold-plated fixtures,

five appliances, a balcony
overlooking

the empty sea.
when the foundation

is poured,
a hole, small

and insignificant
is plugged up, grey

liquid filling
the burrow.

the former inhabitants
(sadly lacking

building permits)
harden inside

their dwelling
—stone rodents

beneath the shifting
syllables of money

The last seaside sparrow

On June 17, 1987, Ammospiza Maritima, known to the public as "Orange,"died in its cage in Disney World, Florida.

Plastic birds.
Birds carved by indigenous knives, painted
tribal shades, or fluorescent, for the tourists,

with glass or beaded eyes. Birds on poles,
in cages, belled; on molded mechanical nests
; birds with musical bowels, trilling

themes from Disney flicks, cheeps spurting
at a button's dial. Tweety Bird in vaudevilles.
Manufactured feathers in gaudy hues, pasted

with chemicals and glue. Sequined pupils.
Birds on screen, on lengths of string; beaks,
in pretense of hunger, agape.

*

A note,
salt and final,
from the grave at Cape Canaveral,

erases the syllables of the real.

After the brothers Grimm

We're after you again, I hear,
armed with our fear of your dark,
wild ruff, those necessary fangs, that glittering eye

—determined to preserve domesticity with a double-
barreled gun and fire's tamed burn.
(In Arkansas, in 1928, we scorched three thousand acres

of forest bare to oust you, felling two fairytales at once)

Dwindled to a few bands scattered across the wilderness,
you retain the dignity of the fierce.
When you need to eat, it is our domesticity you devour

—a cow or a sheep, or perhaps even that shepherd child
who first cried the lie of your name.

The most deliberate extinction
The Great Auk (1884) by Ketil Ketilsson

The Painter was you, K.K.
This is what sinks the horror-anchor.
It was your boot which drove
The last embryo-auks into absence, your
Hands that clubbed the last mating auks
On their nests, on isolate Elder Island.
This is enough to erupt indignance.
But the fact that you took up a brush,

That you chose the black for the vestigial wings,
Selected the white for the iceberg of feathers
Above the beak, the white for the sharp dot of life
In the eye, then formed a backdrop of rock and sea
For the Great Auk to pose against, proud in its element,
Attuned to the harsh Icelandic salt and wind.

That you signed a beauty you stood outside of, exhibited
A life you were alien from, sold a species as a specimen,

That, K.K., is an art for the blind.

From here to nowhere in 27 years
for the Steller's Sea Cow, exterminated by sailors in 1741 on Bering Island

Some will say simply: *It was hunger*
Shipwrecked, who can fault them?

Naming the island after their dead captain,
the sailors set out to find fauna, on land

or sea, that would fill their salt-logged bellies.
They found you—sea cow of the Sirenia family—

slick and speckled, plump, peaceable, *unafeard*, fond
of slow mating calls that hung above the Pacific

in ripe echoes. A rope lashed to a harpoon served
to fell forty of them a night, the naturalist

who christened them deeming their flesh—
as fine as corned beef, once well-prepared.

*

There is another story however. It narrates
human distaste,
        even hatred, toward other species
who assume our traits, possess innate resemblances.

        Animals with human faces have provoked horror, while
the sea cow, with its ability to copulate in human positions,
        face to face
and with *long, erotic foreplay,* must have driven the sailors

        crazy, stranded a quarter of a century without a woman
in sight—those beautiful, full beasts
        heaving their flanks against the waves
in seeming mockery of their mate-lessness.

        Perhaps they sought revenge for this injustice and,
when the waters were purged of elephantine grace, felt
        relief for a moment
—alone with only the ocean's sexless fish.

Devotion
Hibiscus liliflorus, extinct 1982

The object of adulation is limbless.
A scarcely-living stake.
All its blood-blooms siphoned into cloths,
ciboria, transmuted into tinctures
for fear's congregation. Drop by drop,

the flower-flesh vanished—from devotion,
a sense of piety. Jairus's daughter revives.
Lazarus breaks wide the finality of stone.
(The myth miracles weave tenaciously)
Take from me and eat for this is my...

Nothing inside the fence but forms
of absent worship: invocations, coins,
candles. Wax obscuring the charred sandal.

Sear-marks of kisses. Who would know that once,
before the skull, there was a bloom? The flower,

but for its name, extinct as Christ on the cross.

O'o (an extinct Hawaiian honeycreeper bird)
for Aimé Césaire

Trapped in the machine, the infant face of Narcissus
                    sings—
can you hear the cloak of King Kamehama?

             8 000 fingers
             plucking
             80 000 feathers

                    —a soft and hidden harp.

Where nests collapse inside their emptiness
                              like fruit
Where nests become derelict like old men
                              without briefcases
Where nests cave inward like parcels
                              being wrapped
Where nests become eyes without the patronage
                              of eyelids

     in the name of research a red
     incessant pulse like the heart of a hummingbird
                              flickers.

     Where are you kept alive?

     In mating dances reserved for question marks
In copulations claimed by ellipsis
          In a fertility that only the machine's one egg of sound

     contains.

     And the bird?

I've seen it flying through my mind
                        toward its final heartbreak
lured by its own isolate voice
                        sputtering through the speaker's crevices
something leaping
                        like continuance   in its breast

But who answers for this
                        who answers?

Where did they go?
after Loren Eiseley's "Why did they go?"

The Hawaiian honey eater, whose gold and red feathers
    adorned headgear, where did it go? Or *Cylindraspis*,
a Mascarene tortoise, broad enough across to be a dance floor,

yet drilled open by the thousands for cooking oil.
    Where did they go—those island flyers and crawlers,
dreamers of the forty-hour day and panchromatic skies?

And the Falklands fox, victim of the fur trade and myth
    whose extinction was predicted by Darwin, or
the Dawson cariboo, hunted into absence for its pelt.

                    What path did they take through the woods
                    and in what last den lie down?

Where is now the question   not why or how
    (Evidence enough has been given for the human foot and hand,
the gut and god-churched mind.)

    There is little mystery behind who
poisoned the caracara or cut the Pacific snail's shrubbery down

            But where are their blueprints now?

If there is no deity raging over these wrecked creations,
    gathering these extinctions like so many sheep
                    back into the fold,

then where did they go?

A giant storehouse in the universe? A galactic cast-off bin
    where all the original plans persist
though the spark that set their measurements to flesh
                        has been snuffed.

Where *Vorompatra maximus* is a ten-foot sketch, a one-dimensional
    flightlessness, the lines of its hugeness shaky with awe,
its pencilled form fading rapidly along with all
                        the necessary question marks.

27

Litany

For a fad in feathers
in eighteenth-century milliners' shops
                the Carolina parakeet

For feline-prowess
in a mouseless lighthouse
                the Stephen's Island wren

For Mr. Odell's crackshot
                the Jamaican yellow macaw

For Ketil Ketilsson's
left boot
                the last Great Auk

For the palate of emperors
                the auroch

For the hunger of sailors
                the Stellar's sea cow

For the ravaging of forests,
the despoiling of beaches,
the tainting of waters
                the Rapa snail, the Israeli gerbil
                and the hare-lipped suckerfish

For the cultivation of machinery
in rock quarries
                a tiny wild pansy and other
                statistics of rootlessness

The names of birds
on a line by Margaret Avison

It is when a species has been left behind
that it is christened with a human name
our Adam's lexicon locked in the mind

like the passenger pigeon, last of its kind,
dubbed Martha and raised to dubious fame
what, if you name, you're unable to find

or the two parakeets at the end of their line
one of them Incas, and the other one Jane
more Adam's lexicon locked in our minds

and Orange, the sparrow, who lost her own time
pent in a cage amid Disneyfied same
what, if you name, you're unable to find

Constant baptisms we cannot rescind.
Caught in our terrible craving to tame.
That Adam's lexicon locked in our minds
What, by naming, we're unable to find.

Genesis of an Inhumanist

Robinson Jeffers (1887-1962)

Late in your father's life, you lived.
Never quite child in the new sense of the word
But solitary, polyglot, Wordsworthian wanderer
With a keener hawk-knowledge.
Schooled in unreal cities, it was stone
That taught you form, Carmel's ocean
Strafing the eternal cliffs that claimed a tidal
Repetition for the long breakered rhythms of your lines.
Immured with Una and your sons
Yet wide to the winds and stars,
Your world spun inhuman permanence
In an age whose deities are transient.
In Tor House, alone with Tiresias,
You scrawled in the space between lists
Words on the distance of blindness
Never for an instant indifferent
To the salt and rock that is human
Without the familiarity of comfort.

A little too abstract, a little too wise, it is time for us to kiss
the earth again

after the first snow
                sunders
human colours, speed at which
                                machinery
travels, a text luxates beneath
                                        the crust,
cardboard bone, laminate

                        *

a book entitled Earth
                erupting
beneath the scrim
                numerical data pertaining to
swaddled in greens
                & blues,
topographies of human
                value
the word earth   (letters/tubers)
        an oracle obvious
        yet: disposable.

                        *

on the earth itself, enfolding growth
in shrunken topsoil through the erratic
western winter,
                a text settles
squat with graphs & charts
                objective collections
it cannot hear the worm's waking
nor
        (being a book called Earth)
                                does it want to.

                        *

but someone   has cast
     the text   down
       (this is the important act)
a litter of data known as Earth
upon the earth itself
its slow, uncollatable seasons.
someone   has laid the book
beneath the snow   and said to it -
    grow carrots   *provide shade*
     smell of daisies   *become loam*
then tell me   what you know   about earth.

Man dissevered from the earth... often appears
atrociously ugly... the greatest beauty is organic wholeness

The morning bird
    and the morning car
begin their separate melodies
    at the same time

as song evolves from its opposite.

We want to say—either the one
    or the other   shall exist

but if the bird   sings solo   (on magnolia limb or hidden
    in a lilac bush)

human sounds   are conjured

and if cars   should pass   in absence

        (over tarred alleyways
        or around tortured corners)

then the mind   adds a bird.

We think the city depends on its machinery   to endure

    but it does not—

        it relies on its birds.

The beauty of man is dead, or defaced and sarcophagussed
under vile caricatures; the enormous inhuman beauty goes on

1.

Derelict,
the truck
has spent many seasons
                    reversing into earth
Rust widening its rain's eyes
on side panels
                    rims of missing tires
The tailpipe shudders with the silk-smoke of webs
Small life tunnels into the machine's nest
                    Vines clasp steel
A berry's green rubble ripens against the mirror -
                    objects all closer than they appear.

2.

On the corner of Hastings, a man sells carvings. The wood gleams
with other species. He has hung each piece carefully on a tarp
draped upon a steel fence, encircling a vacant lot. We can see
but one human face behind the fence behind the tarp behind
the heron held in wood, beak sutured by the sale price.

3.

Why stop there? said Ronald McDonald
to the Jehovah's Witness
who agreed
one thinking of the world
and the other the earth

both concluding   in a similar deafness
to the Canada Goose

                    sounding an opening
                    outside of ownership.

Mind like a many-bladed machine
subduing the world with deep indifference

When bark becomes inanimate

When trunk becomes steel, cement, plastic

Inanimate as flesh

Then you can grind your mind against it

Your mind's hard ends

Unconscious of doors

Grinding.

Beneath the bark

Sap furthers your life

Air repeats its happening

Out of ashes

Your blind-knived gesture

Annealing

As it utters

Indifferently

In depth

Erase the lines; I pray you not to love classifications; the
thing is a river

The dead sparrow darkens in my palm.
     Whoever names me makes nameless themselves.
Take the word *nature* and recall the directions its sound
                                        falls.

                    *

On landscape in Canadian poetry, there are 1053 entries:
     the principal arrangement is by type (tree, seacoast, flower,
sky, river, city

                            and so on.

                    *

Moment-child the man cried–*I saw five hummingbirds in the back yard!*
     I pray you not to love a sound closing.
The boy who finds the robin in the distance

will inherit the wilderness   (*vast, hideous and desolate*
     saith William Bradford on glimpsing the New World)
A space that is green

can be filled (flesh wrenching flesh is an act
     often
          deemed
               sustainable

One people, the stars and the people, one structure

You said the stars were flesh
founded
on faith
yet not in God (too conforming a gesture)

this silence
    one edifice   the face of a woman
         grown cataract with sirens
             the splintering of seasons
                            this silence

By saying the stars were flesh
you did not imply
transience
or *take & eat for this is my body* (a bleating of sheep)

this silence
    one building   the limbs of a man
         grown numb with steel
             the twisting of daytime
                            this silence

When you say the stars
are flesh
your eyes light upon your own
as if willing it to become
as stars (pure & hard, at a distance)

this silence
    one structure
        Pigeon Park & Hawk Tower
  a galaxy
        recurrent & tender
                            this silence

A photo of Jeffers in mid-life

Older

irony set in your eye, a ranginess in your frame
cigarette gripped like another bone between the laughing-
death of your hands

Younger

Una still alive - hawk-jawed, ascetic-lined, Greek
in your flesh - you sit, legs crossed at your desk, spurning
Oedipus with poems

Yet it is what lies between these moments...

Mid-life

and stone, glinting in the hard-backed sun, arms
firm with Tor House, a vein rising like a rhythm
on your fierce, inhuman skin.

Inviolable

Jeffers was a dervish, perfectly centered & composed, whirling with knives in his hands

—James Karman

Violence in the morning & visions
over Point Lobos and the stark Carmel cliffs
whose ocean bore like hawksong into stone

You wrote

Violence in the waning & stone
from which shapes served as tindered visions
whose breaking at the curve of the cliffs

You wrought

Violence in the evening & cliffs
in which faces engaged with stone
whose features fevered like visions

You walked

*

In the night then violence was not.

*Mourning the broken balance, the hopeless prostration of the
earth under men's hands and their minds*

On the road to the university,
                men march with signs.
In each yellow diamond, a stag rears,
                silhouette of fierceness.
These are daguerreotypes from the future
                where only ancestry's outline
                                remains.

                        *

On the walls of caves
stick etchings of stags
                record past hunts
                                inscribe a kind of wish list.

Yet there is homage
in these ochre figures
                an eating that leaves intact
                                what is beyond us.

                        *

Stags, dripping with ink
traverse
                the blind curve
and where cars
                won't stop
a darkness
                swallows their windshields.
Those who escape
                enter the forest on hind feet
to mate mutely
                with other images.

                        *

Into one silhouette,
          we pour both hope and the fear of flesh
while readying ourselves

for roads & roads around emptiness
          when shadows in yellow diamonds
will suffice for the inhuman

and other shadows   will represent our race.

To see the human figure in all things is man's
disease; to see the inhuman god is our health
Burns Bog Rally, Vancouver Art Gallery, Jan 28, 2000

Even those who have lived amid the bog's
     sphagnum and dwarf pines, seen
the vole's thin skull as a sign of slow vanishings,

even they cannot speak for the inhuman.

Reasons given for the protection of this urban
     wilderness—heritage, resources,
the absorption of fuel—*are* reasons, yet reasons

narrow salvation to statistics and mirrors.
     Is it not enough to say—the sandhill crane—
as one child dared, and leave it at that?

Let the human evolve from that point alone—
     the dark nest,
               unfathomed.

Confession

I am become Jeffers's nemesis:

my mind not stone but flesh
my body not hawk but sand
enchained to acts of lesser innocence.

Rising,
        I do not stride to a tower.

In the afternoon,
        I build no monoliths.

At night, I desire not cliffs
                but dance halls.

Perhaps like my father, spartan & indomitable,
                you measure me little
                        but failure.

Or like the saviour you never wanted
                to become
for you alone was your end, unrepeatable
                in form;

my mouth stuttering the gist of it
        out of flesh & sand.

Confession #2

I am become Jeffers's characters: Tamar

    dreaming trivially
        while her thighs plot fires,
    the Reverend Barclay nailed to his self-love

    like a sick hawk, or the nowhere-rider,
California, gripping the stallion's slick flanks.

And while sometimes I am the Inhumanist
    hurling the axe
        into the deepest trenches

of the sufficient ocean, I am never the ocean itself,
    salt-barnacled and motioning endlessly
        to the land—*come, give yourself.*

It is this gesture I would be for Jeffers:
    a character in the sand
    unreadable to any
    but the wave.

The life of modern cities is barren of poetry because it is not
a lasting life and is lived among unrealities
(An argument in fits & starts)

C'mon Robin, here
        your arched gesture
falters
        a little, humanly

but not, altogether, forgivable

(Sandburg's steel fences, Pound's crowded metro
        not
                poetry?

                        *

O, Robin, you
        loathed the stink of industry, noise
and the necessity of wearing a hat (invitations fobbed off with this
        most pale excuse)

So how could Prufrock's coffee spoons connote anything
        like time
in terms your hawk-mind
        would concede to...

                        *

Because the eye has no vista ready-bound
But must break& break the asphalt like ragweed
To sear forth a stem: a line.
Is this Robin, why the word *barren?*

(But beauty's sieve, in the city, must be finer...

                        *

48

And yet Robin, I
    understand how a rhythm's faith
    can waver amid

plastic trees, painted salmon, rock hewn from styrofoam
    and other such shadows...

*

A city is a city is a city is a city
    for you, Robin, maker of stark statements

made to awaken the masses. But to charge
    the borders so harshly?

(Even between the stalls of a parking lot's erasure, seeds
    split
    in victory
    beneath the sun...

In Limbo

Suspended

Landscapes of waiting. Knowing not what
                    will plummet,
                              what descend and when.

An intimacy with the sphere of last
night's rain, sutured to the spine of a leaf.
To the leaf as it loosens at the socket.
To the spine of an umbilicus.

          What curse for those who poise
     over the city and refuse its tragedies, refuse
          to slide the bright key into the crack of the machine?

Césaire railed against doing's wreakages—

     Heia for those who have never tamed anything!

          The incessant tagging of forests, tankers
          blurring in the bay, trains slitting the same
          skinned route, advertisers baying unbroken.

A child's reflection on a pond   contains nothing of ripple or stone.

          Wise maybe to suspend.

          Our signatures
               far too similar
                    to wounds.

Meditations on wild & tame

Bracken. Dandelion. Burr.
All not purchased in a named packet
called *weed*, destroyed with a violence
reserved for dark thoughts.
Pesticides. Asphalt. Trowel.
They crack through, mutate, return
Nonetheless.

*

For some, chicken sleep on styrofoam,
whales are paid performers, monkeys
exist solely for our needles and language

and wilderness is a space *hideous and desolate.*

*

Annie Dillard, recounting a sea lion's nuzzle of wet-
gold whiskers on her exposed forearm, its slump like an
infant into her soft curve of sleep,

said, *here, on the Galápagos Islands, all
the animals are tame.* Tame, because unfearing,
because not yet broken by the hunger of humans?

Then wilderness must be terror's interpretation.
Or to be tame is an existence on the furthest cusp of wild.

*

We live in a world expunged of forms fierce,
                                        unyielding.
Gone are the giant crickets.

      Moa.   Mastadon.

The eerie tuatara with its tri-pupilled stare.

No mountains and one salamander,
one fiddle tune.

Sameness is the smallest allotment

Blindness constructs the cage.

*

Bacon's Eden of numeric animals, Adam
     as clockmaker, paradise as capital's
highest accrual
    refuse to be reconciled
with childhood's Elysium in which names

     were gentle things.

The stone lions I used to speak to, the bees'
                 embrace
knew nothing of such divisions, nor I of cold
                and sting.

*

I need a wilderness that screes
      at the outskirts of language.

A tame that unfleshes
      in one slow-ocean's breathing.

Eating salmon, knowing un-need

The scene we have set for demise
    is simple: a table laden
with the immortal spices of Egyptians,

the endless viands of Englishmen, the Native's
    copious salmon (so thick
with leaping as to seem a bloom beside riverbanks).

A table fashioned from the far-reaching sweep of forests,
    eternally green, fragrant and fellable.
A scene played out by supermarkets and their replenishable

shelves, aisles stocked with more myths than can ever
    be sold. To our minds, this table is infinite,
and though not all humans may sit, there will always

be beasts for our dishes, unextinguished
                   and seasoned to taste.

Harvest
against the farming of salmon

Making every life a crop, the tanks
three rows of five apiece, screened
and crammed with fish, their army-

hued bodies fertilized in racks, twenty
thousand to each honeycombed compartment.
Larger, they are hemmed in pools, fenced

with electrified steel and fed—themselves—
three times a day. Once, their weir-caught
parents had waited to lay, not at the water's

mouth, as at a quest's conclusion, but
cramped in human dams, in holding cells.
Killed to give birth to captivity, their bellies

squeezed with gloved certainty, eggs
pouring forth, translucent—a wildness
for seeding the tame.

Stanley Park Zoo, Vancouver, BC, circa 1977

Popcorn boxes like felled circus tents
        tumble on the asphalt circuit. Hot chestnut
vendors huddle behind their carts.
        A persistent watery light
waives the particular season.

Dreaming of distant icicles, coat
        the hue of furred urine,
the polar bear paces his trough, claws

transcribing the cement   while hordes
        of barbed wire faces peer incuriously at him
as though down
                        a dry well.

Apes conduct tight brachiations on metal boughs, fondling
                        the last feeling in their genitals,
grinning.

        Slipping again and again down the garish plastic slide
like gumballs with coin-generated speed, penguins,
                        in chlorinated glory.

Otters dive for pennies.   Seals loll quaintly on their sides,

                        as fat as live cigars.

(Stench of hay and herring, sounds of children wanting,
                        taste of stains
                                and waiting)

Just outside the ring of cages, to the cheer of endless spectators,
        whales erupt like fireworks,
                        every hour
                upon the hour.

Easter Island, circa 1500 AD

Nothing but stone idols, toppled.
Earth's memorized rhizomes

suspend the seed's puncture.
Inside the fireless pits, a murmur,

as of seasons, cinders, then darkens
like a neglected language. No different

hunger transformed this land of trees
to grass millennia, ancestorless.

Around the single ring of coastline,
the ocean nods, comatose. Bird-voids

wing the whipped air. In cavities of bone,
a word, cannibalized, lingers, translatable

to those not tourists on the soil.

The Exclusion Act, 1999

Literacy has separated us from the earth
                                    —Max Oelschlaeger

The unbroken script elaborates its calligraphy across the land

    : in the big block letters of fields

    : in the factories' clumsy narratives

    : in the sleek belles-lettres of buildings

    : in the smoothest machine's rhetoric

No one's signature scars the dotted line.

No other species inhabit this text.

    Deciphering its intent
            causes fatal outbreaks of homelessness.

First lines
from Loren Eiseley's Notes of an Alchemist

*A beaver's skull is something not many people see
anymore,* living in cities where the only bones bared
are buildings and the secret of talismans
lies buried beneath the asphalt's muck

*yet a pheasant came into my apartment yard
Sunday,* and sometimes a hawk will hover
over the pear tree or a flicker with its band of darkness
stop by with a cry cold as time

*while along the edge of the airfield between jet
blasts,* mice fidget in hollows, beetles roll their meals
down small declivities, seeds roil in the steam
of innumerable pollinations.

And how do you expect to achieve anything
if you forget the beaver's skull, the pheasant
who nests on flagstones, the jet blasts
entering the hollows?

First lines [2]

The water striders row on a film of water
small pulsations precisely getting Nowhere
shadows a square's unconnected borders
the only live silence on the comatose creek.

*

The ways of the wild are queer but why?
Something in the way they forage in hunger,
the circling of their tracks away from danger,
and their still, irrefutable language of here.

*

There is a sweet-smelling bush in the front yard
like a mecca for bees. And a hollow for rainwater
in my disrepaired path. Besides my absence,
these are my only gifts.

*

There is one animal who never stops
but relentlessly pursues the earth
as if it felt a terrible homelessness
and a hunger for the face of its footprints.

First lines [3]

I sometimes dream of death as a huge
white python, teeth tusked like that Stone Age
tiger long extinct (except in dreams) and sometimes
death is simpler, a fall of snow upon my mind
or a mouse skirmishing in my ear.

I used to carry a frayed rope in my hand to remind
me of how the distance unravels between these scenes—
I found it in a gravel pit—coiled innocent and neglected,
a symbol (or something simpler) for the passage of acids
and dreams and took it with me everywhere. Besides

the shoe-button lion, you see, skulls of owl and beaver,
the last butterfly shuddering on the python's coil,
I have thrown memory away on careless things.

Epiphany
for John Muir, naturalist

Traveling for days through the mind's
monochromatic swamp   perhaps months
          —no sound to chart the time—

grimy,
          stumbling   caught

in a stricture of grey, maps inarticulate.

How many have felt this way?

          :explorers, steeped in endlessness

like Muir   whose landscapes
          stretched into the infinite.

No wonder he fell
                    to his knees and wept when,
on the nth day of unknowing,

                    a flower crept onto his retina:

sturdy at the side of the murk, pistils brilliant
          yellow, petals iridescent

                    —a perfect image of mercy,

indelible life
                    on a terrain in which such gifts
                                        are rare.

Burnt poppy
for W.S. Merwin

Before you bloom, flame

I have spoken many times while you

remain silent. Who bent low

as though to breathe but snuffed instead

that un-folding.

Dark face. Dark eye in no-face

is what you've become.

Dark enough to burn

Without weeping.

I've waited many years to send up my towering,
desperate flower

—Primo Levi

Of those remaining, two have been crushed.

Three have been relegated to an enclave

Beneath the bridge where the dark stunts

Their growth. One has been plucked in momentary

Awe. One cast on the path, roots running like old

Blood between stones. Two have been set inside

Glass urns, their beauty incubating, untouched.

Of those remaining, the last is still unfound.

the sunlit sea supports nothing but the shadows
cast by the outstretched wings of birds

—Guillaume Apollinaire

Supports nothing.
Not this boat, aluminum vessel, nor our bulk:
rods, a bucket of tackle, life jackets
whose zippers are broken.

It cannot satisfy our lust for killing
        (the salmon swim at ever greater depths
        as our technology tentacles to reach them...

The surface opens—the silken erasure of waves
releases a colder passage.
A world inhospitable to *us* begins (like keys left in doors,
        hooks provide a kind of light...

As we have become accustomed, the sea
can no longer support us.
Only the shadowed flight of birds
finds respite on the surface—*outstretched*—
but oh so gently above us.

Slippage

search, birds, search, for the site of your nests in this high
memory, while it is still murmuring

—Jules Superville

There is a bird who frequents ruins
as though seeking the nests of ancestors

and, paying homage to a twigged lineage,
passes the hours by flitting from one false

tree to another. From one steel tree, to one
rigged with wire, to another stuccoed

with sap pallid as the glue of cities, before
it settles on a tree as real as a cemetery, and

preening, selects flowers, singing above
the roots of machinery inside the earth.

There is a bird who opens ruins with its beak,
like nuts in a season sharply being invented, and

slipping through the loopholes of speech and metal,
holds court in both worlds to keep the wild

from the amnesia of builders and its eggs
as warm as ghosts.

Progress

The minatory rat—
      one sure species among thousands teetering
on the lip of absence
      —lies, a short crawl from the compost,
                        crushed.

At first, a final snarl opened a red-dark pasture
      between its teeth, then wheel after
                    wheel

it lost death, became flatter, flayed
      until now it too is part of the alleyway,

the rat-fabric passage.

The naturalist
for John James Audubon (1785-1851)

Who can fault him, in an age when so many species
were felled for far lesser aims? Greed and fashion
    signed many more death warrants than Audubon's

ambition: to travel the continent and paint the unique
variety of birds he found. A self-styled frontier man
    he sported chaps and a gun, was proud of being

a *crackshot* while still appalled by the waste he observed
on the coasts he walked, auks clubbed by the thousands
    for fish bait, drunkards crushing curlew's eggs

in their stumbles beneath the cliffs. With his briefcase of brushes
plucked from geese and foxes, he passed years around lakes
    and marshes, pegging off select pairs of birds

to depict differences in marking. Carrying the bodies back
to his makeshift studio, he would pose the corpses on a grid,
                         contorting
    them into tableaus with wire, adding their lost niches later

from memory. Ballets he made from these birds, and
                        battles—the Labrador
Duck balancing *en pointe*, caught in a *grand jette* off earth's surface,
    the falcon fending its prey from a rival, a perfect hourglass

of blood teetering from the hook of its beak. When these dramas
were complete, he always fixed his signature in the corner in elegant
    curlicues—*Drawn from Nature*—serenely effacing the bullets

and the assistants, the distance and the stuffed, dusty skins.
Now, when
many of these birds are extinct, we could affix such a signature to
everything, each of our acts subtracting from nature

to an extent unimaginable to Audubon, as he strode the planet
paying homage to flight, lithe and inexhaustible
as a third Adam.

The last Canadian poet?
In memory of Al Purdy (d. April 21/00)

> *"Extinct and endangered species sounds like a limitless subject to me,*
> *one that I've been interested in myself"*
>
> —from a letter, March 14/00

Receiving your last letter
    cramped in the quiet, discomforting script of someone

who is dying: a bed-written lexicon of dashes & slants,
                               I cried.

It might be problematical if I wrote you another time,
                        you began.

*

Brusque as an Arctic Rhododendron, you once vanished
to the basement for a tome on Auden while
Eurithe cut the string on the pot roast
as though for a feast inaugural & recurrent.

*

It was she who held your books like ancient weights, balanced
    in
Safeway bags, tallied
           at tables
                in the Railway Club, lugged
                      from taxi
                          to train

(Her arched, discerning gaze, hands pressed, prayer-less
    the last time I heard you read...

*

The last time I heard you read it was of rivers—a litany
        rhythmic & effacing—
the places that had been your body, not solely
        where your body had been.

                        *

With Ameliasburg & the mattress factory,
                        the army & homemade beer
there was a mind as large as this country,
                        traveler
in its Dorset-lost darkness, recollecting
                        forever
the brother dead in the womb & the guilt-soft burden of mothers.

Yet you would call this an Idiot's Song,
                        I think, or say *goddamn,*
acerbic to the end but
                        I thank
you anyway for gold hairs:
                snail horns:
                and the ivory thought in your words—

                ever-warm, unextinct.

The Found

Paean

bird-without
the world
would not be worth
the being
song-suffered
stricken with the silence
of doing, us-noises
only deepening
the desire-need for birds,
their sweet, space-full
singing
in small, reminder-signs
of green.

The honeycomb of lungs

Bees
build around our breathing.
They imitate the arrangement of alveoli
to construct their honeycombs:
                    waxen rooms
                              for their hexagonal dreams
                              and their brood's hum

and this persual of pollen, endlessly,
over the shrinking fields.
In the centre of it all,
                    the dripping sacs heave,
                              the comb's cummerbund expands,

a breath freights the world.

Could these be the rooms prepared for us?

                    (all the while we look up and up
                    when the shimmering cells, so closely,
                    encircle us and honey steams from them...

Bee

you
are fat here, fed
on the silence of an island
that seems immune.

your flight is singular:
no recent divorce precipitates,
no children's voices blur
the lines you navigate

between the troughs of flowers.
your body translates pollen
from this lexicon of blooms
to a fusion.

Our human wish is summed up
in this—your concentric whizz
around our heads,
haloing.

Anatomy—for spring

the bee clambers
inside the swollen, sloped petals of the unplanted holly-
hock
—a second obscured
        but for the way the flower pulses finely
beneath its skin
        the throb of pollen
                        loosening
—a heart inside a lung.

                    *

watch how the bee bores into the node
of the flower and the flower withdraws a little
to receive it and only as much movement
as a breeze occurs as pollen bursts softly
from the wound.

                    *

spawn of sunlight,
bees toss among phlox & laburnum, legs

furzed with pollen like the raised
eyes of braille

—yet unreadable—like their dances
which still annotate the blueprints for their distant

inhuman hives.

Law-breaker

butterfly,
    jay-walking
between lanes of relentless traffic: white

flitter dipping below hoods, buoyed up
    again by the harsh
breeze of rush hour,

                traversing

the instant
    with a brief, brave foray across
inhospitable
    fields of asphalt.

Hastings Street
    alters its momentary pattern
to include
    the wings of a counter-rhythm: butterfly

crossing in a weave
    between cars, its beat binding us all,
with deeper data,
    to the world.

Insect shadows

waterbug

    archaic skater
    velocipedic shadow
    skirs the shallow creek

spider

    sporeless dandelion
    your shadow of precision
    a child's snapped pin-wheel

ant

    economical
    blot, tid-bit of shadow
    not quite buried beneath

The arrest

In the garden,
    alive with night,
a snail rouses
    in the rose blossoms.

The grain of its shell
    unsutured by rain (in places), fractured (as shadow
by light), yet
    coiling an inexorable hull

that heaves and rolls
    like an eye in spring's wet socket.
Through petals—the earth's
soft strata—its slender lengthening

eases—not slowly, but in the holes of its multiple
    homes (this knowing)—sleekly, with
tiny, coded taps at the worn-pink rims—the black
    dew of its eyes, beaded on antennal tips, flickering

with a moist quiet as—from one sprawled
    bloom to the next, in a petalled
sense of leverage—its tinny threads
    linger, globed by dew, then later,

        dried—

            untraversable pathways
              between the stamens

Passage

As if from a fissure in the horizon
        this black life flying

marks evening
        more than the timed shudder of streetlights.

So little in the city speaks inhumanly
        that this tasseled mass of wings
tracing over buildings

        to dusk's thin roost

takes on ritual, mystery.
    (Though they are harsh with their calling above us,
these thousand dark others sent to wake us

        from our sleep.

Easter

The second coming
    is the geese returning—

would be no more miraculous
    than this calling   from the cold recesses of an inhuman

firmament.

    A holy coldness—it lodges in my flesh

as I strain
    eyes up to catch a glimpse   (no more or, eclipse-like, it
                blinds me)

    —this surge of birds strung tidal across the sky,
        thousands of unreadable wings, throats cold with
                                instinct, seeking

no stable

    but a wilderness.

Eclipse

From penumbra
to penumbra
a lifetime passes.
You wait, eyes trained
on the pitted surface as it reddens, pasting
an eerie light on the streets: exquisitely slow.
Over one edge, the earth's darkness heaves,
one *giant leap* holding the moon still,
pinned by a shadow that grinds its tread
over the glow, until, for a time, it is extinguished,
caught in the umbra of our planet, spinning
in its rare position.
The moon,
when it emerges, has one tip
dipped in black, then the whole
lilied sphere is revealed, your awe
enabled by darkness
(believe it)
the first flints of radiance,
singeing.

Admonishment at Boiling Reef, Saturna Island, BC

Foghorns crosshatch the grain of sea.
Gulls fly from the grey like fog embodied,
beaked with a cry cold as the stone lace of cliffs.

A last seal like a silver wick
slits through the kelp beds as a wedge of light
levers the sky's shale weight.

Ocean-flesh, slow in unseen heat, breaks
the city with its breath until it is just one more
movement among mysterious many.

When you return, think lightly.

Notes

Antenatal (a memo)

Dodo, extinct 1790, Reunion Isl.; Auroch, extinct 1627, Poland; Bison bonasus, extinct 1927, Europe; Hare-lipped sucker fish, extinct 1873, Ohio; Cretan owl, prehistoric era Greece; Passenger pigeon, extinct 1914, Cincinnati; Mammoth, prehistoric era Europe; Heath hen, 1932, Massachusetts.

Source: Balouet, Jean-Christophe and Eric Alibert. *Extinct Species of the World*. New York: Barron's, 1990.

Robinson Jeffers: Born in 1887 in Pittsburgh, Jeffers was the son of a Presbyterian minister and a church organist. Schooled in Latin and Greek at Swiss boarding schools, Jeffers later studied astronomy, physiology and forestry before becoming a published poet in 1911. He married Una Call Kuster in 1913 and they moved to Carmel in 1914 where he built Tor House and, later, Hawk Tower, from stones hauled up from the beach. The years spanning the two World Wars were spent in planting a forest, raising his twin sons and writing numerous narratives, lyrics and verse dramas, among them *Tamar* (1920), *The Woman at Point Sur* (1925), *Thurso's Landing* (1931) and *Give your Heart to the Hawks* (1933).

His poetry was continually controversial due to its anti-modern approach, its themes of incest and violence, and its expression of an Inhumanist philosophy in which humanity is often configured as a detrimental aspect of the earth's "transhuman magnificence." Although Jeffers's work had fallen into obscurity by the time of his death in 1962, in recent years it has received a revived interest, particularly in terms of its relevance to the study of literary ecology.

"Genesis of an Inhumanist" draws lines from Jeffers' poems in order to seek the mysterious correspondences which exist between his philosophy and our present, ecologically disastrous reality, as well as between his poetic practice and my own.

Source: Hunt, Tim ed. *The Collected Poetry of Robinson Jeffers*. Stanford: Stanford UP, 1988.

Annie Dillard: Naturalist author of *Pilgrim at Tinker Creek*

Loren Eiseley: d. 1977. Anthropologist author of *The Star Thrower, Notes of an Alchemist*, and *The Innocent Assassins*.

John Muir: Transcendentalist naturalist who crusaded for the preservation of national parks, such as Hetch Hetchy Valley, in the late nineteenth/early twentieth century.